DAWSON CITY

Books LLC®, Reference Series, Memphis, USA, 2011. ISBN: 9781156052259. www.booksllc.net. Copyright: http://creativecommons.org/licenses/by-sa/3.0/deed.en

Table of Contents

Dawson City
Bonanza Creek 1
Dawson City 2
Dawson City Airport 5
Dawson City Nuggets 5
Dawson City Water Aerodrome......... 6
St. Paul's Anglican Church (Dawson City, Yukon) 6
Tr'ondëk Hwëch'in First Nation 6

People from Dawson City
Faith Fenton 7
Fred Berger (politician) 8
George Black (Canadian politician).... 8
Geraldine Van Bibber 9
Isadore "Ike" Bayles 9
James Collisson 10
Jan Eskymo Welzl............................. 11
Joe Juneau (prospector) 11
Joseph Francis Ladue 12
Joseph W. Boyle 12
Kathleen Rockwell 13
Martha Black 13
Nellie Cashman 14
Pierre Berton 15
Robert MacArthur Crawford 16
Robert W. Service 17
Sam Steele 21
Victor Jory 23
William Judge 23
William L. Walsh 24
William Ogilvie (surveyor) 24

Introduction

Purchase of this book entitles you to a free trial membership in the publisher's book club at www.booksllc.net. (Time limited offer.) Simply enter the barcode number from the back cover onto the membership form. The book club entitles you to select from hundreds of thousands of books at no additional charge. You can also download a digital copy of this and related books to read on the go. Simply enter the title or subject onto the search form to find them.

Each chapter in this book ends with a URL to a hyperlinked online version. Type the URL exactly as it appears. If you change the URL's capitalization it won't work. Use the online version to access related pages, websites, footnotes, tables, color photos, updates. Click the version history tab to see the chapter's contributors. Click the edit link to suggest changes.

A large and diverse editor base collaboratively wrote the book, not a single author. After a long process of discussion and debate, the chapters gradually took on a neutral point of view reached through consensus. Additional editors expanded and contributed to chapters striving to achieve balance and comprehensive coverage. This reduced the regional or cultural bias found in many other books and provided access and breadth on subject matter otherwise little documented.

Bonanza Creek

Bonanza Creek is a watercourse in Yukon Territory, Canada. It runs for about 20 miles (32 km) from King Solomon's Dome to the Klondike River. In the last years of the 19th century and the early 20th century, Bonanza Creek was the center of the Klondike Gold Rush, which attracted tens of thousands of prospectors to the creek and the area surrounding it. Prior to 1896 the creek was known as **Rabbit Creek**. Its name was changed by miners in honor of the millions of dollars in gold found in and around the creek.

During gold-mining operations, the course of the creek changed drastically. It was heavily developed during the early 20th century, but was largely abandoned by the 1950s. A handful of small gold-mining operations continue on the creek, but today it is best known for its historic value. The government of Canada has established a historic site centered on one of the gold dredges brought in during the mining years.

Gallery

Discovery Claim at Bonanza Creek

Discovery Claim at Bonanza Creek

Gold panning at Bonanza Creek

Source (edited): "http://en.wikipedia.org/wiki/Bonanza_Creek"

Dawson City

The **Town of the City of Dawson** or **Dawson City** is a town in the Yukon, Canada.

The population was 1,327 at the 2006 census. The area draws some 60,000 visitors each year. The locals generally refer to it simply as 'Dawson', but the tourist industry generally refers to it as 'Dawson City' (partly to differentiate it from Dawson Creek, British Columbia, which is at Mile 0 of the Alaska Highway).

History

Yukon Hotel

The townsite was founded by Joseph Francis Ladue and named in January 1897 after noted Canadian geologist George M. Dawson, who had explored and mapped the region in 1887. It served as the Yukon's capital from the territory's founding in 1898 until 1952, when the seat was moved to Whitehorse.

Dawson has a much longer history, however, as an important harvest area used for millennia by the Hän-speaking people of the Tr'ondëk Hwëch'in and their forebears. The heart of their homeland was Tr'ochëk, a fishing camp at the confluence of the Klondike River and Yukon River, now a National Historic Site of Canada. This site was also an important summer gathering spot and a base for moose-hunting on the Klondike Valley.

The Klondike Gold Rush started in 1896 and changed the First Nations camp into a thriving city of 40,000 by 1898. By 1899, the gold rush had ended and the town's population plummeted as all but 8,000 people left. When Dawson was incorporated as a city in 1902, the population was under 5,000. St. Paul's Anglican Church built that same year is a National Historic Site.

The population was fairly stable until the 1930s, dropped after World War II when the territorial capital was moved to Whitehorse and languished around the 600-900 mark through the 1960s and 1970s, but has risen and held stable since then. The high price of gold has made modern mining operations profitable, and the growth of the tourism industry has encouraged development of facilities. In the early 1950s, Dawson was linked by road to Alaska, and in fall 1955, with Whitehorse along a road that now forms part of the Klondike Highway. In 1978, another kind of buried treasure was discovered when a construction excavation inadvertently found a forgotten collection of more than 500 discarded films of fragile nitrate filmstock from the early 20th century that were buried in and preserved in the permafrost. This historical find was moved to Library and Archives Canada and the US Library of Congress for both transfer to safety filmstock and storage.

The City of Dawson and the nearby ghost town of Forty Mile are featured prominently in the novels and short stories of famed American author Jack London, who lived in the Dawson area from October 1897 to June 1898. One of the books it's been featured in is the beloved book The Call of the Wild.

Geology

Dawson City lies at the western end of the Tintina Fault. This fault line has created the Tintina Trench and continues eastward for several hundred kilometres. Erosional remnants of lava flows form outcrops immediately north and west of Dawson City.

Climate

Like most of the Yukon, Dawson City has a subarctic climate. The average temperature in July is 15.6 °C (60 °F) and in January is −26.7 °C (−16 °F). The highest temperature ever recorded is 34.7 °C (94 °F) on May 31, 1983 and the lowest temperature ever recorded is −55.8 °C (−68 °F) on February 11, 1979. It experiences a wide range of temperatures surpassing 30 °C (86 °F) in most summers and dropping below −40 °C (−40 °F) in winter.

The community is at an elevation of 320 m (1,050 ft) and the average rainfall in July is 48.4 mm (1.9 in) and the average snowfall in January is 24.2 cm (9.5 in). Dawson has an average total annual snowfall of 160.0 cm (63.0 in) and averages 90 frost free days per year. The town is built on a layer of ice, which may pose a threat to the town's infrastructure in the future as the permafrost melts.

City or town

Most of Dawson's buildings look old-fashioned; all new construction must follow this policy.

Klondike Kate's Restaurant

Dredge No. 4

Dawson was incorporated as a city in 1902 when it met the criteria for "city" status under the municipal act of that time. It retained the incorporation even as the population plummeted. When a new municipal act was adopted in the 1980s, Dawson met the criteria of "town", and was incorporated as such, although with a special provision to allow it to continue to use the word "City", partially for historic reasons, partially to distinguish it from Dawson Creek, a small city in northeastern British Columbia. Dawson Creek is also named in honour of George Mercer Dawson. This led the territorial government to post the following signs at the boundaries of the town: "Welcome to the Town of the City of Dawson".

Law and government

In 2004, the Yukon government removed the mayor and the town council, as a result of the town going bankrupt. The territorial government accepted a large portion of the responsibility for this situation in March 2006, writing off $3.43 million of the debt and leaving the town with $1.5 million still to pay off. Elections were set for June 15, 2006. John Steins, a local artist and one of the leaders of the movement to restore democracy to Dawson, was acclaimed as mayor, while 13 residents ran for the 4 council seats.

The government of Tr'ondëk Hwëch'in First Nation, now a self-governing First Nation, is also located in Dawson.

Industry

Today, Dawson City's main industries are tourism and gold mining.

Gold mining started in 1896 with the Bonanza (Rabbit) Creek discovery by George Carmack, Dawson Charlie and Skookum Jim Mason (Keish). The area's creeks were quickly staked and most of the thousands who arrived in the spring of 1898 for the Klondike Gold Rush found that there was very little opportunity to benefit directly from gold mining. Many instead became entrepreneurs to provide services to miners.

Starting approximately 10 years later, large gold dredges began an industrial mining operation, scooping huge amounts of gold out of the creeks, and completely reworking the landscape, altering the locations of rivers and creeks and leaving tailing piles in their wake. A network of canals and dams were built to the north to produce hydroelectric power for the dredges. The dredges shut down for the winter, but one built for "Klondike Joe Boyle" was designed to operate year-round, and Boyle had it operate all through one winter. That dredge (Dredge No. 4) is open as a National Historic Site of Canada on Bonanza Creek.

The last dredge shut down in 1966, and the hydroelectric facility, at North Fork, was closed when the City of Dawson declined an offer to purchase it. Since then, placer miners have returned to the status of being the primary mining operators in the region.

Besides Tr'ochëk, Dawson is home to several national historic sites many of which are included in the Dawson Historical Complex.

Sports

Every February, Dawson City acts as the halfway mark for the Yukon Quest International Sled Dog Race. Mushers entered in the event have a mandatory 36-hour layover in Dawson City while getting their rest and preparing for the second half of the world's toughest sled dog race.

According to the Canada 2006 Census:
- Population in 2006: 1,327
- Population in 2001: 1,251
- Change 2001 to 2006 population change (%): 6.1
- Total private dwellings: 768
- Population density per square kilometre: 40.9
- Land area (square km): 32.45

Transport and communications

Ferry for Highway 9.

Paddlewheeler *Keno*

- Airports: Dawson City Airport, located 8 nautical miles (15 km; 9.2 mi) east of the town, has a 5,000 ft (1,524 m) gravel runway. Dawson City Water Aerodrome is located next to the community on the Yukon River. Both are classified as an airport of entry and, as such, can handle aircraft with up to 30 passengers. The water aerodrome is one of only two in Canada that that is able to handle aircraft with more than 15 passengers.
- Road: Klondike Highway (Yukon route 2) from Whitehorse-open year-round; Top of the World Highway (Yukon route 9) and Taylor Highway (Alaska route 5) from Tok, Alaska.
- Winter transportation: During the winter, Dawson City is accessible via snowmachine or dog sled. The Yukon Quest sled dog race uses Dawson as the midway point of its competition in February.
- Rail: none
- Boat: none except for the Highway 9 ferry at the north end of town, although the Yukon River is navigable (when not frozen solid) and historically was travelled by commercial riverboats to Whitehorse and downstream into Alaska and the Bering Sea. Holland America Line also operates a catamaran, *The Yukon Queen II*, daily (roundtrip) between Dawson City and the town of Eagle, Alaska. This is mainly a service for its package tour customers, though anyone may purchase a ticket for the trip.
- Television: local transmitters for Aboriginal Peoples Television Network (CH4261 channel 9) and CBC Television (CBDDT channel 7, rebroadcasting CFWH-TV)
- Radio: CFYT-FM 106.9 (local community station, rebroadcasts CKRW Whitehorse when not originating local broadcasts); local transmitters for CBC Radio One (CBDN AM 540, rebroadcasting CFWH), CHON-FM (VF2049 90.5FM)
- Newspaper: no daily newspapers locally, *Klondike Sun* published every two weeks, *Yukon News* is available two days per week
- Cable television: municipal government-owned system with several channels via satellite
- Telephone/Internet: Northwestel telephone exchange, with ADSL Internet; also dial-up internet from Yknet; cellular service to be introduced during late 2006 or spring 2007
- Electricity: Yukon Energy Corporation (hydro from the Mayo, Yukon dam, diesel back-up)

Notable people

Dawson City is home of the Berton House Writers' Retreat program, housing established Canadian writers for four three-month get-away-from-it-all subsidized residencies each year. Berton House was the childhood home of popular-history writer Pierre Berton, and is across the street from the cabin that was home to poet Robert W. Service, and the cabin that housed writer Jack London during his time in the town is now just up the street. The London cabin was originally on Henderson Creek, a tributary of the Stewart River where Mr. London spent part of the winter 1897-98.

Dawson City was the starting place of impressario Alexander Pantages. He opened a small theatre to serve the city. Soon, however, his activities expanded and the thrifty Greek went on and became one of America's greatest theatre and movie tycoons.

Pierre Berton narrated the 1957 film *City of Gold* which describes the excitement of Dawson City during the gold rush. Pierre Berton also wrote the book "Klondike", a historical account of the gold rush to the Klondike 1896-1899.

The city was home to the Dawson City Nuggets hockey team, who in 1905 challenged the Ottawa Silver Seven for the Stanley Cup. Travelling to Ottawa by dog sled, ship, and train, the team lost the most lopsided series in Stanley Cup history, losing two games by the combined score of 32 to 4.

Martha Black, the second woman elected to the Canadian House of Commons, as a single mother in Dawson earned a living by staking gold mining claims and running a sawmill and a gold ore-crushing plant. She later married George Black, Commissioner of Yukon, and in 1935 was elected to the House of Commons for the riding of Yukon as an Independent Conservative taking the place of her ill husband.

William Judge, a Jesuit priest who during the 1897 Klondike Gold Rush established a facility in Dawson which provided shelter, food and any available medicine to the many hard-at-luck gold miners who filled the town and its environs.

William Ogilvie, a Dominion land surveyor, explorer and Commissioner of the Yukon, surveyed the townsite of Dawson City and was responsible for settling many disputes between miners. Source (edited): "http://en.wikipedia.org/wiki/Dawson_City"

Dawson City Airport

Dawson City Airport (IATA: **YDA**, ICAO: **CYDA**) is located 8 NM (15 km; 9.2 mi) east of Dawson City, Yukon, Canada, in the Klondike River valley, and is operated by the Yukon government. It has a terminal building and like most airports in its class, the runway is not paved. The gravel runway is 5,006 ft (1,526 m) long and at an elevation of 1,215 ft (370 m). A number of studies have recommended moving the airport or realigning the runway as it is in a narrow mountain valley.

The airport is classified as an airport of entry by NAV CANADA and is staffed by the Canada Border Services Agency. CBSA officers at this airport currently can handle aircraft with no more than 15 passengers.

Source (edited): "http://en.wikipedia.org/wiki/Dawson_City_Airport"

Dawson City Nuggets

Dawson team in Ottawa, 1905 for their challenge

The **Dawson City Nuggets** (also known as the *Klondikes*) were a hockey team from Dawson City, Yukon Territory, Canada that challenged the reigning champion Ottawa Hockey Club, aka "The Silver Seven," in January 1905, for the Stanley Cup. They suffered the most lopsided single-game defeat in the history of Stanley Cup play.

Sponsored by the Klondike entrepreneur Joseph W. Boyle from men of the mining camps during the tailend of the Yukon gold rush, the Nuggets travelled an epic month-long voyage by dog sled, approximately 600 km from Dawson to Whitehorse, narrow gauge rail from Whitehorse to Skagway, ship from Skagway to Vancouver, and train from Vancouver to Ottawa in time for the games. The team had only one bonafide player, ex-Ottawa star Weldy Young, but he was unable to make it to Ottawa in time, delayed in Dawson City as an election official. Exhausted by the trip and without Young, they lost the first game of the two-game total goal series 9-2, and the second 23-2, in which Ottawa star Frank McGee set a record that still stands by scoring fourteen goals (see Ottawa vs. Dawson City). The team then played a series of exhibition games in the east before returning to the Yukon.

Michael Onesi, a Whitehorse newspaper columnist, speculated, shortly before a 1997 re-enactment (see below), that, had the Dawson team triumphed, they would have had the longest dynasty in Stanley Cup history. Challenges normally took place in the cup-holder's town, and visiting teams could not effectively play, the columnist wryly commented, after the brutal journey by overland coach to Dawson, their bodies blacker than a hockey puck from all the bruises of a dog-sled ride.

The challenge

The Nuggets participated in perhaps the most famous Stanley Cup challenge of all, against the Ottawa Hockey Club, aka "The Silver Seven" in 1905. Dawson City had two former elite hockey players, Weldy Young who had played for Ottawa in the 1890s and D.R. McLennan who had played for Queen's College against the Montreal Victorias in the challenge of 1895. Other players were selected from other Dawson City clubs. Dawson City's challenge was accepted in the summer of 1904 by the Stanley Cup trustees, scheduled (inauspiciously) for Friday, January 13, 1905. The date of the challenge meant that Young had to travel later as he had to work in a federal election that December, and meet the club in Ottawa.

To get to Ottawa, several thousand miles away, the club would have to get to Whitehorse by road, catch a train from there to Skagway, Alaska, then catch a steamer to Vancouver, and a train from there to Ottawa. On December 18, 1904 several players set out by dogsled and the rest left the next day by bicycle for a 330 mile trek to Whitehorse. At first the team made good progress, but the weather turned warm enough to thaw the roads, meaning the players had to walk several hundred miles. The team would spend the nights in police sheds along the road. At Whitehorse, the weather turned bad, causing the trains not to run for three days, causing the Nuggets to miss their steamer in Skagway. The next one could not dock for three days due to the ice buildup. The club would find the sea journey treacherous, causing seasickness amongst the team. When the steamer reached Vancouver, the area was too fogged in to dock, and the steamer docked in Seattle. The team from there caught a train to Vancouver, and finally left Vancouver on January 6, 1905, arriving in Ottawa on January 11.

Despite the difficult journey, the Ottawa squad refused to change the date of the first game, only two days away. Otherwise, Ottawa was hospitable. The Klondikers received a huge welcome at the train station, had a welcoming dinner, and used the Ottawa Amateur Athletic Club's rooms for the duration of their stay. Young would not arrive in time to play for Dawson.

The first game started well for Dawson, being only down 3–1 at the half, but things turned ugly afterwards. Norman Watt of Dawson tripped Ottawa's Art Moore, who retaliated with a stick to the mouth of Watt, who promptly knocked Moore out hitting him on the head with his stick. The game ended 9–2 for Ottawa. The game left a poor taste in the Klondikers, complaining that several goals were offside.

Watt then made the mistake of saying that Frank McGee wasn't that good, as he had only scored one in the first game. McGee would score 4 goals in the first half of the second match and 10 in the second half, leading Ottawa to a 23–2 win. Despite this high score, the newspapers claimed that Albert Forrest, the Dawson City goalie, had played a "really fine game," otherwise the score "might have been doubled." Ottawa would celebrate by hosting Dawson at a banquet, after which the players would take the Cup and attempt to drop-kick it over the Rideau Canal. The stunt was unsuccessful, and the Cup landing on the frozen ice, to be retrieved the next day.

The news got worse for McLennan and Watt. The day after the second game, the Yukon Territory announced that they would be laid off from work, effective immediately, albeit with pay until June 30, 1905. The pair worked in the gold commissioner's office.

1997 re-enactment

A team from Dawson competed against the Ottawa Senators alumni, in a re-enactment of the 1905 match, this time at the Corel Centre, complete with organ music, spotlights, and other pizzazz. The Dawson team managed a slight improvement in score: 18-0, with 25 shots-on-goal. 45 percent, the Senators' take of receipts, was contributed to the Heart Institute, while the Dawson team donated 25 ounces of gold, or the cash equivalent, to the Yukon Special Olympics, another 45 percent of the receipts. The rest was designated to Yukon Minor Hockey.

The team symbolically recreated the trip to Ottawa, though train service no longer runs between Whitehorse and the Pacific coast.

Source (edited): "http://en.wikipedia.org/wiki/Dawson_City_Nuggets"

Dawson City Water Aerodrome

Dawson City Water Aerodrome (TC LID: **CEG7**) is located adjacent to Dawson City, Yukon, Canada and is open from August to September.

The airport is classified as an airport of entry by NAV CANADA and is staffed by the Canada Border Services Agency. CBSA officers at this airport currently can handle aircraft with no more than 30 passengers. It is one of only two water aerodromes in Canada, Dryden Water Aerodrome is the other, that is able to handle aircraft with more than 15 passengers.

Source (edited): "http://en.wikipedia.org/wiki/Dawson_City_Water_Aerodrome"

St. Paul's Anglican Church (Dawson City, Yukon)

St. Paul's Anglican Church is an historic Carpenter Gothic style Anglican church building located on the corner of Front and Church streets in Dawson City, Yukon, Canada. Built of wood in 1902, it once served as the cathedral of the Anglican Diocese of Yukon until the diocesan see was moved to Whitehorse in 1953. Its steep pitched roof, its pointed arch entry through its belfry tower and its lancet windows are typical of Carpenter Gothic churches. St. Paul's is a National Historic Site of Canada as designated by the Government of Canada on June 1, 1989.

St. Paul's is still an active parish in the Diocese of Yukon. The Rev. Dr. Lee Titterington is its incumbent priest, while the Rev. Percey Henry is its deacon.

Source (edited): "http://en.wikipedia.org/wiki/St._Paul%27s_Anglican_Church_(Dawson_City,_Yukon)"

Tr'ondëk Hwëch'in First Nation

The **Tr'ondëk Hwëch'in** ([t'oⁿdək hwətʃ'in]; formerly the **Dawson Indian Band**) is a First Nations located in the central Yukon, Canada. Its main population centre is Dawson City, Yukon.

Many of today's Tr'ondëk Hwëch'in, or people of the river, are descendants of the Hän-speaking people who have lived along the Yukon River for thousands of years. They traveled extensively throughout their traditional territory harvesting salmon from the Yukon River and caribou from the Fortymile and Porcupine Herds. Moose, small game, and a variety of plants and berries provided additional food sources. Other raw materials needed to make tools, clothing and shelter were procured from this diverse and rich environment. The Hän traded with neighboring First Nations people and maintained interrelations through family connections and frequent gatherings.

In the mid-19th century, European fur traders and missionaries established a presence in the territory. Contact with the newcomers presented new challenges and opportunities for the Hän. Trade increased and new goods and economic practices were introduced. The Hän used a combination of traditional and newly introduced skills, goods and materials to maintain their survival and assist the newcomers.

In the 1880s gold was discovered in the Ch'ëdäh Dëk, or Fortymile River, area – a site used by the Hän as a caribou interception point and grayling fishing spot. In 1896 more gold was discovered near Tr'ochëk, at the confluence of the Yukon and Klondike Rivers. The Klondike River hosted abundant salmon stocks and the Hän had an encampment at Tr'ochëk that was used seasonally for hundreds of years. The ensuing rush brought thousands of people to Tr'ochëk and surrounding areas.

Recognizing the influences that the newcomers would have on his people, Hän leader Chief Isaac, worked with the Government of Canada and the Anglican Church to move his people from Tr'ochëk to Moosehide – 5 km (3.1 mi) downriver at 64°05'40"N 139°26'12"W. Chief Isaac was respected among his own people and newcomers alike. While he welcomed the stampeders, "he never failed to remind them that they prospered at the expense of the original inhabitants by driving away their game and taking over their land." Chief Isaac envisioned the impact that new lifestyles would have on Hän traditional culture. In response he entrusted many songs and dances to First Nations people living in Alaska.

During the years following the Klondike Gold Rush, the Hän worked to find a balance between their traditional lifestyle and the ways of the newcomers.

Yukon First Nations set the Land Claims process in motion during the 1970s. Tr'ondëk Hwëch'in began negotiating their individual Land Claim in 1991. The Tr'ondëk Hwëch'in Final Agreement was signed on July 16, 1998 and came into effect on September 15, 1998.

The government is growing and evolving to support citizens in ensuring a strong and healthy future while maintaining connections to traditional knowledge and the land. Promoting the Hän language, learning traditional skills from the Elders, and investing in youth have all strengthened Tr'ondëk Hwëch'in development. This respect for their heritage and dedication to the future is reflected in a variety of ways. The biennial Moosehide Gatherings, the establishment of Dänojà Zho Cultural Centre, the designation of Tr'ochëk National Historic site, and the return of the traditional songs, which were once entrusted to Alaskan First Nations people, all reflect Tr'ondëk Hwëch'in investment in their future and pride in their rich heritage.

Source (edited): "http://en.wikipedia.org/wiki/Tr%E2%80%99ond%C3%ABk_Hw%C3%ABch%E2%80%99in_First_Nation"

Faith Fenton

Faith Fenton in 1880

Alice Freeman (1857 - 1936), better known by her pseudonym, **Faith Fenton**, was a Canadian school teacher and investigative journalist. She became Canada's first female columnist while writing for the Toronto Empire. Freeman wrote under the pseudonym *Faith Fenton* to keep her job as a teacher, as journalism was seen as an unacceptably disreputable activity for a teacher to be involved in. With the low salary she earned at these jobs, she required both salaries to support herself.

Childhood

Fenton was the third of twelve children, and was sent to live with a Bowmanville, Ontario minister and his wife when Fenton was age ten. Margaret Reike, her foster mother ensured Fenton got an education beyond what her parents might have afforded.

Journalism career

Fenton began her journalist career in 1886 as a Toronto correspondent for the *Northern Advance*, a daily newspaper in Barrie, Ontario. In 1888 she began writing a column for *The Toronto Empire*. The column, titled *Women's Empire*, dealt with issues relevant to women of the day: sexual discrimination, sexual harassment, child abuse and wage disparity. Fenton wrote columns at night, travelled to work as a journalist during the summer, while remaining a teacher during the day. As a writer, she interviewed famous people of the day like Susan B. Anthony, Oliver Wendell Holmes, Catherine Parr Traill, Pauline Johnson and Emma Albani. She kept her double-identity secret until 1893. She resigned her job as a schoolteacher in 1894, and became a full-time journalist.

When gold was discovered in the Yukon, Fenton accompanied the Yukon Field Force's nurses to the Yukon as a correspondent for *The Globe*. Fenton departed Toronto in the spring, arriving in the Yukon in August. In the Yukon, Fenton met and married Dr. John Brown. Fenton took up residence in Dawson City and began to send reports of the gold rush back to eastern Canada. She returned to Toronto in 1904.

Faith Fenton on assignment in the Yukon

Source (edited): "http://en.wikipedia.org/wiki/Faith_Fenton"

Fred Berger (politician)

Fred Berger (1932 – 2009) was a Canadian politician. First elected to the non-partisan Yukon Territorial Council in the 1974 territorial election, he became the first leader of the Yukon New Democratic Party when the territory adopted political parties for the first time in the 1978 election. Berger was not elected to the Yukon Legislative Assembly, however, losing to Meg McCall in the Klondike electoral district.

He remained leader of the party until 1981, when he was succeeded by Tony Penikett. He later operated a number of businesses, including a movie theatre and a drug store, in Dawson City, but remained a prominent activist within the party until his death in 2009.

Source (edited): "http://en.wikipedia.org/wiki/Fred_Berger_(politician)"

George Black (Canadian politician)

George Black

George Black, PC (April 10, 1873 – August 23, 1965) was an administrator and politician in Yukon, Canada. He went to Yukon in 1898 during the Gold Rush and prospected for gold, making a fortune and losing it when his claim was swept away in a flood. He then established a law practice in Dawson City. He was elected to the Yukon council in 1905, and first ran for the Canadian House of Commons in the 1908 federal election but was defeated.

In the 1911 federal election he was H. H. Stevens' campaign manager, and was rewarded by the government of Robert Laird Borden by being appointed to the position of Commissioner of the Yukon. As Commissioner from 1912 to 1915, he tried to bring in legislation to protect miners, loggers and others who worked for companies that went bankrupt.

During World War I, Black recruited a regiment from the Yukon to fight in the war. He became the company's Captain, and was wounded in combat.

Following the war, he settled in British Columbia in 1919, and ran unsuccessfully for a seat in the Legislative Assembly of British Columbia.

He first won a seat in Parliament in the 1921 election as a Conservative. As a Member of Parliament (MP), he introduced legislation to give Yukoners the right to trial by jury and to protect mining titles.

After the Tories won the 1930 election, the new Prime Minister of Canada, R.B. Bennett, nominated Black to be Speaker of the Canadian House of Commons. As Speaker, he kept a .22 caliber pistol in his chambers which he used to shoot rabbits on Parliament Hill. Black's personal and financial life were strained during the Great Depression and he had a nervous breakdown in the summer of 1934. He went to England where he was committed to a psychiatric hospital. Being unavailable to preside over the final session of the 17th Parliament, he resigned prior to its commencement in January 1935. Since Black was unfit to run in the 1935 election his wife, Martha Black, ran in his place as an "Independent Conservative". She held the seat, becoming the second woman elected to the House of Commons (the first being Agnes Macphail).

Black was released from hospital in 1936, and moved to Vancouver to recuperate. Martha stepped aside, and allowed Black to run for the Yukon seat in the 1940 election. He was returned to Parliament where remained until the 1949 election, which he did not contest.

He attempted to recapture his seat in the 1953 election but was unsuccessful.

Source (edited): "http://en.wikipedia.org/wiki/George_Black_(Canadian_politician)"

Geraldine Van Bibber

Geraldine Van Bibber (born July 3, 1951) was the Commissioner of the Yukon Territory. She is a member of the Gwich'in First Nation.

She was appointed a Commander of the Order of St. John in 2006.

On November 30, 2010, former MLA Doug Phillips was named her replacement.

Source (edited): "http://en.wikipedia.org/wiki/Geraldine_Van_Bibber"

Isadore "Ike" Bayles

Isadore "Ike" Bayles (Hebrew: יצחק ביילעס) (February 20, 1876 – May 31, 1956) was an Alaskan businessman and considered one of the founding fathers of Anchorage, Alaska.

Early life
Isadore Bayles was born in Libau, Courland (Latvia) in 1876. He was the youngest of six children born to Rabbi Ephraim Bayles & Ida Rashe Friedman. Ike was also the brother of Sam Bayles, who brought the first Torah to Alaska in 1900. Isadore lived with his family in Kovno, Lithuania until he left for America in 1891 at the age of 15.

The Klondike Gold Rush
Ike Bayles ended up in the Pacific Northwest, possibly because his older brother Sam, who he had not seen since he was a child in Lithuania, was living in Spokane. In the 1890s Ike was living in Victoria, British Columbia & possibly Seattle. In the summer of 1897, word reached Seattle about gold being discovered in the Klondike River in the Yukon Territory of Canada. This led to the Klondike Gold Rush of 1897-98. Being very business savvy, Ike decided to travel to the Yukon and set up a business selling supplies to miners. In 1898, Ike left for the Klondike. He travelled by boat up the coast of British Columbia arriving in Skagway. From there, he travelled the Chilkoot Trail to Carcross, where he almost died from pneumonia. After resting in Carcross, Ike continued north until he reached Dawson City in the spring of 1899. Ike set up his business in Dawson City selling supplies to the more than 40,000 people that had now reached the area. In 1905, after 6 years of business and a dwindling population, Ike decided to move to Fairbanks, where gold had been discovered a couple of years earlier.

Life in Alaska
Ike Bayles arrived in Fairbanks in 1905 to follow his second gold rush. He set up a clothing business there. In 1909, the Jewish residents of Fairbanks organized themselves into a congregation. They chose the name "Chevra Bikur Cholim", which means "Society for Visiting the Sick." Chevra Bikur Cholim was active in philanthropic works as well as planning Jewish festivals and ceremonies. Ike Bayless was elected President of Chevra Bikur Cholim in 1909.

After becoming President, Ike travelled to New York City to purchase a complete set of books, as well as the Sefar Torah, so the congregation could properly conduct the Jewish services. While in New York, Ike met and married a 17 year old Russian Jew named Beatrice Swartz. Ike then returned to Fairbanks where he awaited the shipment of books which arrived in September 1909. On September 12, 1909, the Jewish community of Fairbanks held a celebration at Eagle Hall to welcome the Sefar Torah and the rest of the books that had arrived from New York.

In 1910, another gold rush started in Iditarod. Ike Bayles left Fairbanks to follow the 10,000 miners in what would be the last great gold rush. Ike met up with his brother, Sam Bayles, (who had also followed the gold rush to Nome, Alaska in 1900) and they opened the Bayles Clothing Company with locations in Iditarod and Discovery, Alaska. In Iditarod, Ike was Chairman of the Fire Committee, City Councilman, a member of the Street Committee and the Law & Order Committee. Ike was also a marshal at the first annual Iditarod Sweepstakes Race on January 11, 1911. It was around this time that Beatrice, Ike's wife, gave birth to their first daughter Edith. In 1912, Ike left Iditarod and traveled to Illinois for a short time where his second daughter Dorothy was born in 1912 or 1913.

Business in Anchorage
Ike traveled back to Alaska in 1914 and ended up at Ship Creek Landing, which would later become Anchorage. The Alaska Railroad had just been established and the area of Ship Creek Landing was designated at its headquarters. At this time, Ship Creek Landing was just a tent city. The population quickly grew to over 2,000 people & Ike saw more potential for business opportunities. Ike sold his two clothing stores in Iditarod & Discovery to a merchant from Flat City named Abe Wiess. Ike then opened a clothing store on the northwest corner 4th Avenue & D Street in Anchorage with his business partner H.N. Jaffe, who owned at least one other clothing store in Ruby, Alaska along the Yukon River. The store was called "Jaffe & Bayles Leading Clothier", and it was one of the first businesses in Anchorage. After many years, he eventually bought out his partner & renamed the store "I. Bayles Clothier." The building remained on 4th street until it was destroyed on March 27, 1964 during the

Good Friday Earthquake. Ike was also elected to the first City Assembly and the School Board of Anchorage during this time. From the 1920s to the 1940s, Ike traveled back and forth from Seattle to Alaska while his clothing store remained in business. He eventually closed his business and retired in San Francisco.

Ike Bayles died on May 31, 1956 in San Francisco from cirrhosis of the liver and heart failure. He is buried in Colma, California.

Currently, at the intersection of 4th Ave. & D Street in Anchorage, D Street is now an alley which is named "Bayles Way."

The ceremonial starting line for the Iditarod Trail Sled Dog Race is directly in front of the location where Ike's clothing store once stood.

Source (edited): "http://en.wikipedia.org/wiki/Isadore_%22Ike%22_Bayles"

James Collisson

James Thomas Joseph Collisson (August 21, 1875 – July 30, 1962) was a politician in Alberta, Canada, a longtime municipal councillor in Edmonton, and a candidate for election to the Legislative Assembly of Alberta.

Early life

Collisson was born in Lucan, Ontario in 1875. He was educated there and in London, Ontario, and moved to Edmonton to teach in 1898. He remained there until 1903, when he moved to Dawson, Yukon. He taught there for two years, and returned to Edmonton in 1905. He joined the law form Short, Cross and Bigger (of which former and future mayor William Short was a partner) as a student at law. He was admitted to the Law Society of Alberta in 1908.

He served on Edmonton's public school board from 1908 until 1913.

Municipal politics

Collisson first sought municipal office in the 1916 municipal election, when he ran for alderman on Edmonton City Council. He finished eighth of eleven, which wasn't high enough to be elected (only the top six candidates were elected in that election). He was more successful in 1920, when he finished fourth of sixteen candidates and was elected to a two year term. He was re-elected in 1922 (when he finished fifth of sixteen candidates) and 1924 (when he finished second of eleven). He cut short his third term in order to run for mayor in the 1925 election, but finished second in a six candidate race as incumbent Kenny Blatchford took more than fifty-five percent of the vote.

He returned to politics in the 1928 election, when he returned to his old position on the strength of a sixth place finish in a fourteen candidate field. He was re-elected in the 1930 election, when he finished third of nine candidates, but left municipal politics for good at the conclusion of this term.

On council, he chaired the finance committee.

Provincial politics

Collisson ran for the Legislative Assembly of Alberta as a Liberal candidate in the 1930 provincial election. He finished eighth of seventeen candidates in the riding of Edmonton, and was eliminated on subsequent counts (the riding used a single transferable vote voting system at the time).

Personal life, death, and legacy

After leaving politics, Collisson served as the president of Edmonton's community chest from 1941 until 1948.

James Collisson died July 30, 1962. He was survived by his wife, Irene, one son and two daughters, and eight grandchildren.

Source (edited): "http://en.wikipedia.org/wiki/James_Collisson"

Jan Eskymo Welzl

Jan Eskymo Welzl - statue in Zábřeh.

Jan Welzl (15 August 1868, Zábřeh, Moravia - 19 September 1948 Dawson, Canada) was a Moravian traveller, adventurer, hunter, gold-digger, Eskimo chief and Chief Justice in New Siberia and later story-teller and writer. He is known under the pseudonym **Eskymo Welzl** or the nickname **Arctic Bismarck**.

Rudolf Těsnohlídek began to write down his adventures on the basis of conversations with him. Pavel Eisner continued this but did not finish and later Bedřich Golombek and Edvard Valenta completed the work. The book "Třicet let na zlatém severu" (literally "Thirty Years in the Golden North") had great success in Czechoslovakia and also abroad, where people suspected that "Eskymo Welzl" did not exist and that the real author was Karel Čapek who wrote the preface to foreign editions.

The asteroid *15425 Welzl*, discovered on 24 September 1998, is named after him.

Source (edited): "http://en.wikipedia.org/wiki/Jan_Eskymo_Welzl"

Joe Juneau (prospector)

Joseph Juneau

Joseph Juneau (1833 or 1836–1899) was a miner and prospector from Canada who was born in the Quebec town of Saint-Paul-l'Ermite (later renamed Le Gardeur and now incorporated into the city of Repentigny) to François Xavier Juneau dit Latulippe and Marguerite Thiffault Juneau. He is best known for co-founding, with Richard Harris, the city of Juneau, Alaska, United States. The first major gold discovery in Juneau or Douglas Island (across from Juneau) was circa 1880. It has been the political capital of Alaska since 1906.

His Native American guide in southeastern Alaska was Chief Kowee. Kowee is credited with exploring much of the Juneau area. Richard and Joe were sent with Kowee by George Pilz, an entrepreneur and mining engineer from Sitka. Richard and Joe traded with the natives much of their grubstake for hoochinoo. When they returned to Pilz empty-handed, he promptly sent them back to the Juneau area. There, Kowee took them beyond Gold Creek (which today flows beside the city's United States Federal Building) to Silver Bow Basin. Today, a creek on Douglas Island is named Kowee Creek.

After the discovery of gold in Juneau, Richard and Joe loaded approximately 1,000 pounds of gold ore back to Sitka.

The town was originally called Harrisburg or Harrisburgh, and then Rockwell. Miners often called it "'Rockwell' also known as 'Harrisburg'" in their mining records. There was also a proposal to name the town Pilzburg for Pilz. It did not take up its current name until a miners' meeting on December 14, 1881. The name Juneau received 47 of the 72 votes cast while Harrisburg received 21 votes and Rockwell only 4. Joe Juneau reportedly bought drinks for fellow miners to name the city in his honor.

Joe Juneau traveled to Dawson City, Yukon during the Klondike Gold Rush of the 1890s. He usually spent gold as fast as he got it but at the end of his life he owned a small restaurant in Dawson. Juneau died of pneumonia in March, 1899 in Dawson. His body was brought back to the town that bears his name and was buried in the city's Evergreen Cemetery on August 16, 1903.

His cousin Solomon Juneau founded the city of Milwaukee, Wisconsin.

Source (edited): "http://en.wikipedia.org/wiki/Joe_Juneau_(prospector)"

Joseph Francis Ladue

Joseph Francis Ladue (July 28, 1855 – June 27, 1900) was a prospector, businessman and founder of the Dawson City, Yukon. Joseph Francis Ladue was born in Schuyler Falls, New York. His mother died when he was only 7 years old, and his father died in 1874. Upon his father's death, 19-year-old Joe headed West. He worked in a gold mine as a general labourer, engineer, foreman and superintendent. He stuck with that and went prospecting through Arizona and New Mexico. He did not strike it rich and in 1882 he crossed the Chilkoot Pass into the interior of the Yukon. He was prospecting and trading there a couple of years.

In August 1896, a few days after discovery of gold on Klondike, he staked 250 acres (1.0 km) of bloggy flats at the mouth of the Klondike River to Yukon River as a townsite. In January 1897 he named a new town Dawson after Canadian geologist George Mercer Dawson. In July, 1897 about 5000 people lived there. Joe Ladue could sell town lots from $800 to $8000 and he could leave Dawson rich in that year.

He returned to his home town and in December 1897 he married Anna "Kitty" Mason. He came from Yukon rich, but unfortunately in poor health. He died at Schuyler Falls on June 27, 1900.
Source (edited): "http://en.wikipedia.org/wiki/Joseph_Francis_Ladue"

Joseph W. Boyle

Joseph Whiteside Boyle (born 16 November 1867 in Toronto, Ontario, died 14 April 1923 in Hampton Hill, Middlesex, England), better known as **Klondike Joe Boyle**, was a Canadian adventurer who became a businessman and entrepreneur in the United Kingdom.

Boyle was early to recognize the potential of large-scale gold mining in the Klondike gold fields, and as the initial placer mining operations waned after 1900, Boyle and other companies imported equipment to assemble enormous dredges, usually electric-powered, that took millions more ounces of gold from the creeks while turning the landscape upside-down, shifting creeks.

Boyle organized a hockey team in 1905, often known as the Dawson City Nuggets, that endured a difficult journey to Ottawa, Ontario (by overland sled, train, coastal steamer, then transcontinental train) to play the Ottawa Senators for the Stanley Cup, which until 1924 was awarded to the top hockey team in Canada and could be challenged for by a team. Ottawa thrashed the Dawson team.

During World War I, Boyle organized a machine gun company, giving the soldiers insignia made of gold, to fight in Europe. The unit was incorporated into larger units of the Canadian Army.

In July 1917 Boyle undertook a mission to Russia on behalf of the American Committee of Engineers in London to help reorganize the country's railway system. In December 1917 he successfully petitioned the new Bolshevik government of Russia to return archives and paper currency from the Kremlin to Romania. In February 1918 he served the principal intermediary on behalf of the Rumanian government in effecting a ceasefire with revolutionary forces in Bessarabia.

Boyle, in cooperation with Captain George Alexander Hill, a Russian-speaking member of the British secret service, carried out clandestine operations against German and Bolshevik forces in Bessarabia and southwestern Russia. In March–April 1918 he rescued some 50 high-ranking Rumanians held in Odessa by revolutionaries. This made Boyle a national hero in Romania and a gave him influence within its royal court. At the Paris Peace Conference in 1919 he was instrumental in helping Romania to obtain a $25-million credit from the Canadian government.

He was awarded the special title of "Saviour of Romania". He remained a close friend, and was at one time a possible lover of the Romanian Queen, British-born Marie of Edinburgh. On the Queen's behalf, Boyle organized millions of dollars of Canadian relief for Romanians, earning the title of hero. He was decorated for his exploits by the governments of Russia, France, Britain and Romania.

His relationship with the queen remains something of a mystery. Some historians speculated they were lovers and point to a mysterious woman in black who brought flowers to his grave every year on the anniversary of his death in 1923. Queen Marie died in 1938 and nobody appeared at his grave after that year, so it was always thought that she was the mystery woman.

Boyle is presently buried in his Canadian home town of Woodstock, Ontario, after being buried for 50 years in Hampton Hill.
Source (edited): "http://en.wikipedia.org/wiki/Joseph_W._Boyle"

Kathleen Rockwell

Studio portrait of Klondike Kate Rockwell

Kathleen Eloise Rockwell (1873–1957), best known as **"Klondike Kate"**, gained her fame as a dancer and vaudeville star during the Klondike Gold Rush, where she met Alexander Pantages who later became a very successful vaudeville/motion picture mogul. She gained notoriety for her flirtatious dancing and ability to keep hard-working miners happy if not inebriated. She died in obscurity after some minor success training Hollywood starlets in the 1940s.

Biography

Rockwell was born in Kansas and Dakota but grew up in Spokane, Washington. Her stepfather had stature in the community and the family lived in a large mansion. But economic failure created tension in the family, and this lack of home stability echoed throughout Rockwell's sometimes stormy life. She was known as an independent spirit, or "tomboy" as a youngster, often impersonating boys and playing with them rather than with members of her own gender. She seemed a happy child, although felt all too intensely the lack of social mobility for women in the late 19th and early 20th centuries.

Her parents sent the rebellious teenager to boarding school, but Rockwell was expelled. She had little interest for education and spent more time thinking of ways to flout the rules.

In the 1890s, after divorcing the stepfather, Rockwell's mother moved with her to New York. The younger Rockwell here had an unsuccessful attempt at show-biz. She left for greener pastures and arrived in Alaska in 1899. The Royal Canadian Mounted Police held a tight leash on prospective miners and various hangers-on trying to get to the Yukon and find fortunes in gold. Refused entry by a Mountie, she is reputed to have donned a boy's outfit and jumped on a boat headed for the Yukon.

First working as a tap-dancer in Whitehorse, Rockwell found her stride in Dawson City as a member of the Savoy Theatrical Company. Her act was very popular with the miners, and she was dubbed "Klondike Kate" as a result. It was in Dawson that she met Alexander Pantages, at that time a struggling waiter and bartender who eventually rose to become theatre owner.

The intense love affair between Pantages and Rockwell became the stuff of legend in the Yukon, although streaks of jealousy insured that they found more stability in their professional lives than in their personal ones. They were not above swindling unsuspecting miners, and this dubious quality eventually infected their own relationship. She later accused him of reneging on a promise to marry her as well as attempting to cheat her of her money.

In 1902, the Klondike Gold Rush was already dying out and Rockwell headed south, first to British Columbia where she set-up a store-front movie theater and eventually to eastern Oregon, where she seems to have played the part of a recluse and social outcast.

She never achieved any of the fame she briefly held in Alaska, although she made full use of the memories. "Sourdough" reunions in the 1930s provided a measure of uptick in her fame, as did training young Hollywood starlets in the 1940s.

Near the end of her life she married a miner named John Matson, who remained in Alaska as she stayed in Oregon. They were together for 13 years. Her last years were spent mostly as a visible emblem of the bygone Gold Rush. Rockwell died in 1957.

Ernie Pyle has a chapter about Klondike Kate (who he calls Kate Rothrock) in his book *Home Country*.
Source (edited): "http://en.wikipedia.org/wiki/Kathleen_Rockwell"

Martha Black

Martha Louise Purdy Black OBE (February 24, 1866 – October 31, 1957) was a Canadian politician and the second woman elected to the Canadian House of Commons.

Martha Louise Munger was born in Chicago, Illinois, the daughter of George and Susan Munger, a wealthy family. She was educated at Saint Mary's College (Indiana), which was run by the Sisters of the Holy Cross. Of the five children her mother had over four years, Martha was the only one to survive. She had two younger siblings, George Jr. and Belle. Her father operated a laundry that was destroyed in the Great Chicago Fire.

Martha married Will Purdy. He left her to go to Hawaii and Martha broke up with him. In 1899, she gave birth to their child in a log cabin child after he left.

In 1899 she crossed the Chilkoot Pass into Canada, heading for the gold rush in the Klondike (Dawson City, Yukon). She returned home to Chicago, and returned again to the Klondike in 1900.

She earned a living by staking goldmining claims and running a sawmill and a gold ore-crushing plant. In 1904, she married George Black, Commissioner of the Yukon.

In the 1935 federal election, she was elected for the riding of Yukon as an Independent Conservative taking the place of her ill husband. She was the second woman ever to be elected to the House of Commons of Canada.

She published an autobiography, *My Seventy Years*, in 1938. This was subsequent updated and published in 1998 as "Martha Black: Her Story from the Dawson Gold Fields to the Halls of Parliament".

Honours and awards

In 1917, she was made a Fellow of the Royal Geographical Society for her series of lectures on the Yukon that she presented in Great Britain. In 1946, she was made an Officer of Order of the British Empire for her cultural and social contributions to the Yukon.

In 1986 a Canadian Coast Guard high-endurance multi-tasked vessel was given the name *"Martha L. Black"* in her honour. The vessel sails in the Quebec Region area. In 1997, Canada Post issued a $0.45 stamp in her honour. Martha black made a book called the "Gold Rush Pioneer" Martha was a great pleasure!
Source (edited): "http://en.wikipedia.org/wiki/Martha_Black"

Nellie Cashman

Ellen Cashman (1845 – January 4, 1925), better known as **Nellie Cashman**, was a native of County Cork, Ireland, who became famous across the American and Canadian west as a nurse and gold prospector.

Early years

Cashman came to the United States around 1850 with her mother and her sister. She had lost her father a short time before. In 1865, the Cashman girls arrived in San Francisco, California, where they settled a new home.

British Columbia

A few years later, the Gold rush era came, and Nellie, willing to become an adventurous woman, left her family home in 1874, heading to the Cassiar Mountains, in British Columbia, Canada. A lifelong Catholic woman, she set up a boarding house for miners, asking them for donations to be made for the Sisters of St. Anne in return for receiving the services available at her boarding house.

Cashman travelled to Victoria, to deliver 500 dollars received in donations, to the nuns of the Sisters of St. Anne, when she heard that a snowstorm had attacked the Cassiar mountains area, stranding and injuring 26 miners, who were also suffering from scurvy. She immediately organized an expedition with six men and collected food and medicines, planning to find the men and rescue them.

Conditions at the Cassiar Mountains were so dangerous during the time, that not even the Canadian Army considered it a worthy task to try to rescue the twenty six stranded men. When they heard of Cashman's expedition, a commander sent his troops to find her and bring her and her group of men back safely.

An Army trooper found her standing over the ice of Stikine River, cooking her meal for the evening. She offered the trooper and a few other men from his group some tea, and convinced them that it was her will to continue and she would not head back without rescuing the men.

After 77 days of unfriendly weather, she found the sick men, which, as it turned out, were more than twenty six; some estimates put the number of lives that Cashman and her crew saved as many as seventy five men. She used a Vitamin C diet to re-establish the group's health. Thereafter, she was fondly known in the region as the "Angel of the Cassiar".

Arizona

Later on in life, she moved to Tombstone, Arizona, where she kept working for her Catholic faith. She raised money to build the Sacred Heart Catholic Church there, and she worked with the Sisters of St. Joseph's. She also kept her work as a caretaker, getting a job as a nurse in a local Cochise hospital.

After her brother-in-law's death in 1881, Nellie invited her sister, Fanny, to move to Nellie's home in Tombstone along with her five children. However, Fanny died two years later, leaving Nellie as the only caretaker of the five children, whom she came to love as if they were her own children.

Nellie still hoped to find gold someday, and she travelled to Baja California, Mexico, soon after her sister's death, after hearing rumors that gold and silver could also be found there. With 100 miles to reach their destination, Nellie decided that six men would lead the group that she was travelling with, which consisted of Nellie and twenty-one men. After sixteen hours, however, most of the men in the group had suffered dehydration from the Arizona heat. As a consequence, the group's water supply was almost gone. Many historians propose that Nellie and the twenty one men were rescued by Mexicans.

In December of that year, a group of bandits tried to commit a robbery in Bisbee. The robbery went wrong, and many innocents were killed. Five men were captured and taken to trial. They were sentenced to capital punishment; the date of March 28 of 1884 was set for their hanging.

Citizens in Tombstone were very angry at the men that were found guilty, and most of them overjoyed that they would be hanged. Soon after the sentence was announced, sheriff J.L. Ward ran out of courtesy tickets to the event, so a local carpenter built a grandstand next to the courthouse, planning to charge for tickets.

Cashman was indignant at the behavior of the citizens of Tombstone, feeling that no death should be celebrated. She befriended the five convicts, visiting them constantly to provide them with spiritual guidance. She spoke to the sheriff about the upcoming event, pleading with him to put a curfew in place during the day of the hangings so that no crowds would stand by the street to watch. The sheriff conceded, and a curfew was set.

Next, she and some friends went at night to the site of the execution, destroying the grandstand with hammers and axes. While the hangings proceeded as scheduled, the public was unable to watch, and Nellie achieved what she wanted: the five men died feeling that a small portion of dignity had been restored to them.

Later on, she found out that a medical school planned to dig up the bodies of the five convicts, to be used as study corpses. She had two prospectors stay ten nights at the Boot Hill Cemetery, to ensure that the bodies stayed in the graves.

Nellie co-owned and ran a restaurant and hotel in Tombstone called Russ House (now known as Nellie Cashman's). Her partner in this enterprise was Robert Pascholy. According to a popular legend, once, a client complained about Nellie's cooking, and Doc Holliday drew his side arm, asking the customer to repeat what he had said. Embarrassed, the client replied, "Best I ever ate."

In 1886, she left Tombstone to travel all across Arizona, setting restaurants and boarding houses in Nogales, Jerome, Prescott, Yuma and Harquahala, near Phoenix.

Yukon and Alaska

In 1898, she left Arizona for the Yukon, staying there until 1905. This move was once again motivated by her dream of finding gold during the Klondike Gold Rush. She owned a store in Dawson City. She searched for gold in the Klondike, Fairbanks and Nolan Creek.

In 1921, she visited California, where she declared that she'd like to be appointed U.S. deputy Marshal for the area of Koyukuk. In 1922, the Associated Press documented her trip from Nolan Creek to Anchorage.

In 1925, Cashman began suffering from pneumonia and rheumatism. Her friends took her to the same hospital she had helped built 51 years before, the Sisters of St. Anne. Ironically, she died soon afterwards in that institution. She was interred at Ross Bay Cemetery in Victoria, British Columbia.

On March 15, 2006, Nellie Cashman was inducted into the Alaska Mining Hall of Fame.

Source (edited): "http://en.wikipedia.org/wiki/Nellie_Cashman"

Pierre Berton

For other people with the same name, see Pierre Berton (disambiguation).

Pierre Francis de Marigny Berton, CC, O.Ont (July 12, 1920 – November 30, 2004) was a noted Canadian author of non-fiction, especially Canadiana and Canadian history, and was a well-known television personality and journalist.

An accomplished storyteller, Berton was one of Canada's most prolific and popular authors. He wrote 50 books, including ones on popular culture, Canadian history, critiques of mainstream religion, anthologies, children's books and historical works for youth. He popularized Canadian history.

Biography

He was born on July 12, 1920, in Whitehorse, Yukon, where his father had moved for the 1898 Klondike Gold Rush. His family moved to Dawson City, Yukon in 1921, where they lived until moving to Victoria, British Columbia in 1932. His mother, Laura Beatrice Berton (née Thompson) was a school teacher in Toronto until she was offered a job as a teacher in Dawson City at the age of 29 in 1907. She met Frank Berton in the nearby mining town of Granville shortly after settling in Dawson and teaching kindergarten. Laura Beatrice Berton's autobiography of life in the Yukon entitled *I Married the Klondike* was published in her later years and gave her, what her son Pierre describes as 'a modicum of fame, which she thoroughly enjoyed.'

Like his father, Pierre Berton worked in Klondike mining camps during his years as a history major at the University of British Columbia, where he also worked on the student paper *The Ubyssey*. He spent his early newspaper career in Vancouver, where at 21 he was the youngest city editor on any Canadian daily, replacing editorial staff that had been called up during the Second World War.

Berton himself was conscripted into the Canadian Army under the National Resources Mobilization Act in 1942 and attended basic training in British Columbia, nominally as a reinforcement soldier intended for The Seaforth Highlanders of Canada. He elected to "go Active" (the euphemism for volunteering for overseas service) and his aptitude was such that he was appointed Lance Corporal and attended NCO school, and became a basic training instructor in the rank of corporal. Due to a background in university COTC and inspired by other citizen-soldiers who had been commissioned, he sought training as an officer.

Miners and prospectors ascend the Chilkoot Trail during the Klondike Gold Rush

Berton spent the next several years

attending a variety of military courses, becoming, in his words, the most highly trained officer in the military. He was warned for overseas duty many times, and was granted embarkation leave many times, each time finding his overseas draft being cancelled. A coveted trainee slot with the Canadian Intelligence Corps saw Berton, now a Captain, trained to act as an Intelligence Officer (IO), and after a stint as an instructor at the Royal Military College in Kingston, Ontario, he finally went overseas in March 1945. In the UK, he was told that he would have to requalify as an IO because the syllabus in the UK was different from that in the intelligence school in Canada. By the time Berton had requalified, the war in Europe had ended. He volunteered for the Canadian Army Pacific Force (CAPF), granted a final "embarkation leave", and found himself no closer to combat employment by the time the Japanese surrendered in September 1945. Berton moved to Toronto in 1947. At the age of 31 he was named managing editor of *Macleans*. In 1957, he became a key member of the CBC's public affairs flagship program, Close-Up, and a permanent panelist on the popular television show *Front Page Challenge*. That same year, he also narrated the Academy Award-nominated National Film Board of Canada documentary *City of Gold*, exploring life in his hometown of Dawson City during the Klondike Gold Rush. He then released an album in conjunction with Folkways Records, entitled *The Story of the Klondike: Stampede for Gold - The Golden Trail*.

Berton joined the *Toronto Star* as associate editor and columnist in 1958, leaving in 1962 to commence *The Pierre Berton Show*, which ran until 1973. It was on this show that in 1971 Berton interviewed Bruce Lee in what was to be the famous martial artist's only surviving television interview. Berton's television career included spots as host and writer on *My Country*, *The Great Debate*, *Heritage Theatre*, *The Secret of My Success* and *The National Dream*.

Berton served as the Chancellor of Yukon College and, along with numerous honorary degrees, received over 30 literary awards such as the Governor General's Award for Creative Non-Fiction (three times), the Stephen Leacock Medal of Humour, and the Gabrielle Léger Award for Lifetime Achievement in Heritage Conservation. He is a member of Canada's Walk of Fame, having been inducted in 1998. In The Greatest Canadian project, he was voted #31 in the list of great Canadians.

In 2004, Berton published his 50th book, *Prisoners of the North*, after which he announced in an interview with CanWest News Service that he was retiring from writing. On October 17, 2004, the $12.6 million CAD Pierre Berton Resource Library, named in his honour, was opened in Vaughan, Ontario.

He had lived in nearby Kleinburg, Ontario, for about fifty years.

Berton raised eyebrows in October 2004 by discussing his forty years of recreational use of marijuana on two CBC Television programs, *Play* and *Rick Mercer Report*. On the latter show he gave a "celebrity tip" on how to roll a joint.

Death

Berton died at Sunnybrook hospital in Toronto, reportedly of heart failure, at the age of 84 on November 30, 2004.

His childhood home in Dawson City, now called Berton House, is a writers' retreat. Established writers apply for three-month long subsidized residencies there; while in residence, they give a public reading in both Dawson City and Whitehorse. The Berton House Retreat is sponsored by a charitable foundation set up to support it and by the Klondike Visitors Association; the administrator is Elsa Franklin. Franklin was Berton's long-time editor and agent.

Pierre Berton Award

Established in 1994, the Pierre Berton Award is presented annually by Canada's National History Society for distinguished achievement in presenting Canadian history in an informative and engaging manner. Berton was the first recipient and agreed to lend his name to future awards.

Awards

- Queen Elizabeth II Golden Jubilee Medal 2002
- Order of Canada, Companion, 1986.
- Canadian Booksellers Award, 1982.
- Canadian Authors Association Literary Award for non-fiction, 1981
- Queen Elizabeth II Silver Jubilee Medal 1977
- Nellie Award, best public affairs broadcaster in radio, 1978.
- Governor General's Awards for: *The Last Spike*, 1972; *Klondike*, 1958; *The Mysterious North*, 1956.
- Stephen Leacock Medal for Humour, 1959.

Source (edited): "http://en.wikipedia.org/wiki/Pierre_Berton"

Robert MacArthur Crawford

Robert MacArthur Crawford (1899-1961) is known for writing *The U.S. Air Force* song. He was born in Dawson City, Yukon, and spent his childhood in Fairbanks, Alaska. During World War I he attempted to become a pilot in the United States Army Air Service but was dismissed when he was discovered to be underage. He attended the Case Scientific Institute, where he joined the Phi Kappa Psi fraternity. Crawford then enrolled in Princeton University, and graduated in 1925. He later studied and taught at the Juilliard School of Music. Crawford learned how to fly an airplane in 1923. He flew himself around the United States in a small plane to concerts, where he was introduced as "The Flying Baritone." *Liberty* magazine sponsored a contest in 1938 for a musical composition that would become the official song of the U.S. Army Air Corps. Out of 757 submissions, Crawford's was chosen as the winner. During World War II, Crawford flew for the Air Transport Command of the U.S. Army Air Forces. In 1947, Crawford joined the University of Miami's music faculty. He remained there for ten years, until he left to focus on composing.

Source (edited): "http://en.wikipedia.org/wiki/Robert_MacArthur_Crawford"

Robert W. Service

Robert William Service (January 16, 1874 – September 11, 1958) was a poet and writer who has often been called "the Bard of the Yukon".

Service is best known for his poems "The Shooting of Dan McGrew" and "The Cremation of Sam McGee", from his first book, *Songs of a Sourdough* (1907; also published as *The Spell of the Yukon and Other Verses*). "These humorous tales in verse were considered doggerel by the literary set, yet remain extremely popular to this day." *Songs of a Sourdough* has sold more than three million copies, making it the most commercially successful book of poetry of the 20th century.

Life

Commemorative Plaque in Preston, England

Early life

Robert W. Service was born in Preston, Lancashire, England, the first of ten children. His father, also Robert Service, was a banker from Kilwinning, Scotland who had been transferred to England.

At five years old Robert W. Service went to live in Kilwinning with his three maiden aunts and his paternal grandfather, who was the town's postmaster. There he is said to have composed his first verse, a grace, on his sixth birthday:
God bless the cakes and bless the jam;
Bless the cheese and the cold boiled ham:
Bless the scones Aunt Jeannie makes,
And save us all from bellyaches. *Amen*
At nine Service rejoined his parents who had moved to Glasgow. He attended Glasgow's Hillhead High School.

"Service worked in a bank after he left school" ("he joined the Commercial Bank of Scotland which today is the Royal Bank of Scotland"). He was writing at this time and reportedly already "selling his verses". He was also reading poetry: Browning, Keats, Tennyson, and Thackeray.

Service moved to Canada at the age of 21 and travelled to Vancouver Island, British Columbia with his Buffalo Bill outfit and dreams of becoming a cowboy. He drifted around western North America, "wandering from California to British Columbia," taking and quitting a series of jobs: "Starving in Mexico, residing in a California bordello, farming on Vancouver Island and pursuing unrequited love in Vancouver." This sometimes required him to leech off his parent's Scottish neighbors and friends who had previously immigrated to Canada.

In 1899 Service was a store clerk in Cowichan Bay, British Columbia. He mentioned to a customer (Charles H. Gibbons, editor of the Victoria *Daily Colonist*) that he wrote verses, with the result that six poems by "R.S." on the Boer Wars had appeared in the *Colonist* by July 1900 – including "The March of the Dead" that would later appear in his first book. (Service's brother Alick was a prisoner of the Boers at the time, having been captured on November 15, 1899, alongside Winston Churchill.)

The *Colonist* also published Service's "Music in the Bush" on September 18, 1901, and "[[s:The Little Old Log Cabin|The Little Old Log Cabin]]" on March 16, 1902.

In her 2006 biography, *Under the Spell of the Yukon*, Enid Mallory revealed that Service had fallen in love during this period. He was working as a "farm labourer and store clerk when he first met Constance MacLean at a dance in Duncan B.C, where she was visiting her uncle." MacLean lived in Vancouver, on the mainland, so he courted her by mail. Though he was smitten, "MacLean was looking for a man of education and means to support her" so was not that interested. To please her, he took courses at McGill University's Victoria College, but failed.

Down on his luck in 1903, Service was hired by a Canadian Bank of Commerce branch in Victoria, British Columbia, using his Commercial Bank letter of reference. The bank "watched him, gave him a raise, and sent him to Kamloops in the middle of British Columbia. In Victoria he lived over the bank with a hired piano, and dressed for dinner. In Kamloops, horse country, he played polo. In the fall of 1904 the bank sent him to their Whitehorse branch in the Yukon. With the expense money he bought himself a raccoon coat."

Throughout this period, Service continued writing and saving his verses: "more than a third of the poems in his first volume had been written before he moved north in 1904."

Yukon period

Cabin of Robert Service in Dawson City, Yukon *(Photo by Hans-Jürgen Hübner)*

Whitehorse was a frontier town, less than ten years old. Located on the Yukon River at the Whitehorse Rapids, it had begun in 1897 as a campground for prospectors on their way to Dawson City to join the Klondike Gold Rush. The railroad that Service rode in on had reached Whitehorse only in 1900.

Settling in, "Service dreamed and listened to the stories of the great gold rush." He also "took part in the extremely active Whitehorse social life. As was popular at the time he recited at concerts – things like 'Casey at the Bat' and 'Gunga Din', but they were getting stale."

One day (Service later wrote), while pondering what to recite at an upcoming church concert he met E.J. "Stroller" White, editor of the *Whitehorse Star*. White suggested: "Why don't you write a poem for it? Give us something about our own bit of earth. We sure would appreciate it. There's a rich paystreak waiting for someone to work. Why don't you go in and stake it?"

Returning from a walk one Saturday night, Service heard the sounds of revelry from a saloon, and the phrase "A bunch of the boys were whooping it up" popped into his head. Inspired, he ran to the bank to write it down (almost being shot as a burglar), and by the next morning "The Shooting of Dan McGrew" was complete.

"A month or so later he heard a gold rush yarn from a Dawson mining man about a fellow who cremated his pal." He spent the night walking in the woods composing "The Cremation of Sam McGee," and wrote it down from memory the next day.

Other verses quickly followed. "In the early spring he stood above the heights of Miles Canyon ... the line 'I have gazed on naked grandeur where there's nothing else to gaze on' came into his mind and again he hammered out a complete poem, "The Call of the Wild". Conversations with locals led Service to write about things he had not seen (some of which had not actually happened) as well. He did not set foot in Dawson City until 1908, arriving in the Klondike ten years after the Gold Rush when his renown as a writer was already established.

After having collected enough poems for a book, Service "sent the poems to his father, who had emigrated to Toronto, and asked him to find a printing house so they could make it into a booklet. He enclosed a cheque to cover the costs and intended to give these booklets away to his friends in Whitehorse" for Christmas. His father took the manuscript to William Briggs in Toronto, whose employees loved the book. "The foreman and printers recited the ballads while they worked. A salesman read the proofs out loud as they came off the typesetting machines." An "enterprising salesman sold 1700 copies in advance orders from galley proofs." The publisher "sent Robert's cheque back to him and offered a ten percent royalty contract for the book."

Service's book, *Songs of a Sourdough*, was "an immediate success." It went through seven printings even before its official release date. Ultimately, Briggs "sold fifteen impressions in 1907. That same year there was an edition in New York, Philadelphia, and London. The London publisher, T. Fisher Unwin, struck a twenty-third printing in 1910, and thirteen more by 1917." "Service eventually earned in excess of $100,000 for *Songs of a Sourdough* alone (Mackay 14, 408n19)."

(In the United States, the book would be given the more Jack London-ish title, *The Spell of the Yukon and Other Verses*).

"When copies of the book reached Whitehorse, Robert's own minister took him aside to let him know how wicked were his stories. Service hung his head in shame.... But, that summer, tourists from the south arrived in Whitehorse looking for the famous poet; and he autographed many of his books."

"In 1908, after working for the bank for three years in Whitehorse, he was sent outside on mandatory paid leave for three months, a standard practice for bank employees serving in the Yukon." According to Enid Mallory, he went to Vancouver and looked up Constance MacLean. Now that he was a successful author, she agreed to become engaged to him.

Following his leave, in 1908 the bank transferred Service to Dawson, where he met and talked to veterans of the Gold Rush, now ten years in the past: "they loved to reminisce, and Robert listened carefully and remembered." He used their tales to write a second book of verse, *Ballads of a Cheechako*, in 1908. "It too was an overwhelming success."

In 1909, when the bank wanted Service to return to Whitehorse as manager, he decided to resign. "After quitting his job, he rented a small two-room cabin on Eighth Avenue in Dawson City from Mrs. Edna Clarke and began his career as a full-time author." He immediately "went to work on his novel.... He went for walks that lasted all night, slept till mid-afternoon, and sometimes didn't come out of the cabin for days. In five months the novel, called *The Trail of '98*, was complete and he took it to a publisher in New York." Service's first novel also "immediately became a best-seller."

Newly wealthy, Service was able to travel to Paris, the French Riviera, Hollywood, and beyond. He returned to Dawson City in 1912 to write his third book of poetry, *Ballads of a Rolling Stone* (1912). During that time he became a freemason, being initiated into Yukon Lodge No. 45 in Dawson.

It is not known what happened between Service and Constance MacLean. There are no known letters between then from after the time Service went to Dawson City. In 1912 she "married Leroy Grant, a surveyor and railroad engineer based in Prince Rupert."

Later life

Robert Service Memorial, Kilwinning, Ayrshire.

Service left Dawson City for good in 1912. From 1912 to 1913 he was a correspondent for the *Toronto Star* during the Balkan Wars.

In 1913 Service arrived in Paris, where he would live for the next 15 years. He settled in the Latin Quarter, posing as a painter. In June 1913 he married Parisienne Germaine Bougeoin, daughter of a distillery owner, and they purchased a summer home at Lancieux, Côtes-d'Armor, in the Brittany region of France. Thirteen years younger than her husband, Germaine Service lived 31 years following his death, dying at age 102 in 1989.

Robert Service was 41 when World War I broke out; he enlisted, but was turned down "due to varicose veins." He briefly covered the war for the *Toronto Star* (from December 11, 1915 through January 29, 1916), but "was arrested and nearly executed in an outbreak of spy hysteria in Dunkirk." – then "worked as a stretcher bearer and ambulance driver with the Ambulance Corps of the American Red Cross, until his health broke." Convalescing in Paris, he wrote a new book of mainly war poetry, ***Rhymes of a Red Cross Man***, in 1916. The book was dedicated to the memory of Service's "brother, Lieutenant Albert Service, Canadian Infantry, Killed in Action, France, August 1916."

With the end of the war, Service "settled down to being a rich man in Paris.... During the day he would promenade in the best suits, with a monocle. At night he went out in old clothes with the company of his doorman, a retired policeman, to visit the lowest dives of the city.". During his time in Paris he was reputedly the wealthiest author living in the city, yet was known to dress as a working man and walk the streets, blending in and observing everything around him. Those experiences would be used in his next book of poetry, ***Ballads of a Bohemian*** (1921), "The poems are given in the persona of an American poet in Paris who serves as an ambulance driver and an infantryman in the war. The verses are separated by diary entries over a period of four years."

In the 1920s Service began writing thriller novels. *The Poisoned Paradise, A Romance of Monte Carlo* (New York, 1922) and *The Roughneck. A Tale of Tahiti* (New York, 1923) would both be made into silent movies.

In 1930 Service returned to Kilwinning, to erect a memorial to his family in the town cemetery. He also visited the USSR in the 1930s and later wrote a satirical "Ballad of Lenin's Tomb". For this reason his poetry has never been translated into Russian in the USSR and he was never mentioned in Soviet encyclopedias.

Service's second trip to the Soviet Union "was interrupted by news of the Hitler-Stalin pact. Service fled across Poland, Latvia, Estonia and the Baltic to Stockholm. He wintered in Nice with his family, then fled France for Canada." Not long after, the Germans invaded France, and "arrived at his home in Lancieux ... looking specifically for the poet who had mocked Hitler in newspaper verse."

During World War II Service lived in California, "and Hollywood had him join with other celebrities in helping the morale of troops – visiting US Army camps to recite his poems. He was also asked to play himself in the movie *The Spoilers*, working alongside Marlene Dietrich and John Wayne." "He was thrilled to play a scene with Marlene Dietrich."

After the war Service and his wife returned to his home in Brittany, to find it destroyed. They rebuilt, and he lived there until his death in 1958, though he wintered in Monte Carlo on the French Riviera.

Service's wife and daughter, Iris, travelled to the Yukon in 1946 "and visited Whitehorse and Dawson City, which by then was becoming a ghost town. Service could not bring himself to go back. He preferred to remember the town as it had been."

Service wrote prolifically during his last years, publishing six books of verse from 1949 to 1955 (with one more appearing posthumously the following year).

It was at Service's flat in Monte Carlo that Canadian broadcaster Pierre Berton recorded, over a period of three days, many hours of autobiographical television interview, for the Canadian Broadcasting Corporation, in the spring of 1958, not long before Service died.

Service wrote two volumes of autobiography - *Ploughman of the Moon* and *Harper of Heaven*. He died in Lancieux and is buried there in the local cemetery.

Writing

Robert Service wrote the most commercially successful poetry of the century. Yet his most popular works "were considered doggerel by the literary set." During his lifetime, he was nicknamed "the Canadian Kipling." – yet that may have been a double-edged compliment. As T.S. Eliot has said, "we have to defend Kipling against the charge of excessive lucidity," "the charge of being a 'journalist' appealing only to the commonest collective emotion," and "the charge of writing jingles." All those charges, and more, could be levelled against Service's best known and best loved works.

Certainly Service's verse was derivative of Kipling's: "[[s:The Cremation of Sam McGee|The Cremation of Sam McGee]]," for instance, uses the form of Kipling's "Ballad of East and West."

In his E.J. Pratt lecture "Silence In the Sea," critic Northrop Frye argued that Service's verse was not "serious poetry," but something else he called "popular poetry": "the idioms of popular and serious poetry remain inexorably distinct." Popular poems, he thought, "preserve a surface of explicit statement" – either being "proverbial, like Kipling's 'If' or Longfellow's 'Song of Life' or Burns's 'For A' That'," or dealing in "conventionally poetic themes, like the pastoral themes of James Whitcomb Riley, or the adventurous themes of Robert Service."

Service himself did not call his work poetry. ""Verse, not poetry, is what I was after ... something the man in the street would take notice of and the sweet old lady would paste in her album; something the schoolboy would spout and the fellow in the pub would quote. Yet I never wrote to please anyone but myself; it just happened. I belonged to the simple folks whom I liked to please."

In his autobiography, Service described his method of writing at his Dawson City cabin. "I used to write on the coarse rolls of paper used by paper–hangers, pinning them on the wall and printing my verses in big charcoal letters. Then I would pace back and forth before them, repeating them, trying to make them perfect. I wanted to make them appeal to the eye as well as to the ear. I tried to avoid any literal quality."

One remarkable thing about both of Service's best-known ballads is how easily he wrote them. When writing about composing "The Shooting of Dan McGrew," 'easy' was exactly the word he used: "For it came so easy to me in my excited state that I was amazed at my facility. It was as if someone was whispering in my ear." And this was just after someone had tried to shoot him. He continued: "As I wrote stanza after stanza, the story seemed to evolve itself. It was a marvelous experience. Before I crawled into my bed at five in the morning, my ballad was in the bag."

Similarly, when he wrote "The Cremation of Sam McGee,", the verses just flowed: ""I took the woodland trail, my mind seething with excitement and a strange ecstasy.... As I started in: There are strange things done in the midnight sun, verse after verse developed with scarce a check ... and when I rolled happily into bed, my ballad was cinched. Next day, with scarcely any effort of memory I put it on paper."

In 1926, Archibald MacMechan, Professor of English at Canada's Dalhousie University, pronounced on Service's Yukon books in his *Headwaters of Canadian Literature*:
The sordid, the gross, the bestial, may sometimes be redeemed by the touch of genius; but that Promethean touch is not in Mr. Service. In manner he is frankly imitative of Kipling's barrack-room balladry; and imitation is an admission of inferiority. 'Sourdough' is Yukon slang for the provident old-timer ... It is a convenient term for this wilfully violent kind of verse without the power to redeem the squalid themes it treats. *The Ballads of a Cheechako* is a second installment of sourdoughs, while his novel *The Trail of '98* is simply sourdough prose.
MacMechan did give grudging respect to Service's World War I poetry, conceding that his style went well with that subject, and that "his *Rhymes of a Red Cross Man* are an advance on his previous volumes. He has come into touch with the grimmest of realities; and while his radical faults have not been cured, his rude lines drive home the truth that he has seen."

Reviewing Service's *Rhymes of a Rebel* in 1952, Frye remarked that the book "interests me chiefly because ... I have noticed so much verse in exactly the same idiom, and I wonder how far Mr. Service's books may have influenced it. There was a time, fifty years ago," he added," when Robert W.Service represented, with some accuracy, the general level of poetic experience in Canada, as far as the popular reader was concerned.... there has been a prodigious, and, I should think, a permanent, change in public taste."

Service has also been noted for his use of ethnonyms that would normally be considered offensive "slurs", but with no insult apparently intended. Words used in Service's poetry include *jerries* (Germans), *dago* (Italian), *pickaninny* (in reference to a Mozambican infant), *cheechako* (newcomer to the Yukon and Alaska gold fields, usually from the U.S.), *nigger* (African-American), *squaw* (Aboriginal woman), and *Jap* (Japanese).

Recognition

A bust of Service in Whitehorse

Robert W. Service has been honoured with schools named for him including Service High School in Anchorage, Alaska, Robert Service Senior Public School (Middle/ Jr. High) in Toronto, Ontario and Robert Service School in Dawson City, Yukon. He was also honoured on a Canadian postage stamp in 1976. The Robert Service Way, a main road in Whitehorse, is named after him.

Additionally, the Bard & Banker public house in Victoria, British Columbia is dedicated to him, the building having at one time been a Canadian Bank of Commerce branch where Service was employed while residing in the city. In 2010 Phillips Brewery in Victoria released the Service 1904 Scottish Stone Fired Ale, available only on tap in three Victoria locations: The Bard & Banker, Irish Times, and Penny Farthing public houses.

Service's first novel, *The Trail of '98*, was made into a movie by Metro-Goldwyn-Mayer, directed by Clarence Brown. "*Trail of '98* ... starring Dolores Del Rio, Ralph Forbes and Karl Dante in 1929 ... was the first talking picture dealing with the Klondike gold rush and was acclaimed at the time by critics for depicting the Klondike as it really was."

Folksinger Country Joe MacDonald set some of Service's World War I poetry (plus "The March of the Dead" from his first book), to music for his 1971 studio album, *War War War*.

Dawson City cabin

Robert Service lived from 1909 to 1912 in a small two-room cabin on 8th Avenue which he rented from Edna Clarke in Dawson City, Yukon. His prosperity allowed him the luxury of a telephone.

Service eventually decided he could not return to Dawson, as it would not be as he remembered it. He wrote in his autobiography:

Cabin of Robert Service in Dawson City, Yukon *(Photo by Hans-Jürgen Hübner)*

"Only yesterday an air-line offered to fly me up there in two days, and I refused. It would have saddened me to see dust and rust where once hummed a rousing town; hundreds where were thousands; tumbledown cabins, mouldering warehouses."

After Service left for Europe, the Imperial Order of the Daughters of the Empire (I.O.D.E.) took care of the cabin until 1971, preserving it. In 1971 it was taken over by Parks Canada, which maintains it, including its sod roof, as a tourist attraction.

Irish-born actor Tom Byrne created *The Robert Service Show* which was presented in the front yard of the cabin, starting in 1976. This was very popular for summer visitors and set the standard for Robert Service recitations. A resurgence in sales of Service's works followed the institution of these performances.

Mr. Byrne discontinued the show at the cabin in 1995, moving it to a Front Street storefront. Since 2004 the show has been held at the Westmark Hotel in Dawson City at 3:00 p.m. every day during the summer months. Mr. Byrne collects Robert Service first editions, and corresponded with Mr. Service's widow for years.

At the Service Cabin, local Dawson entertainers dressed in period costumes and employed by Parks Canada offer biographical information and recite Service's poetry for visitors sitting on benches on the front lawn. Johnny Nunan performed this role through 2006. The present performer shares his first name (Fred). Following the presentation, visitors can view Service's home through the windows and front door. The fragility of the house, and the rarity of the artifacts, precludes any possibility of allowing visitors to enter the house itself.

Source (edited): "http://en.wikipedia.org/wiki/Robert_W._Service"

Sam Steele

Sir Samuel Benfield Steele, in his uniform as commanding officer, Lord Strathcona's Horse.

Major General **Sir Samuel Benfield Steele**, CB, KCMG, MVO (5 January 1849 – 30 January 1919) was a distinguished Canadian soldier and police official. He was an officer of the North-West Mounted Police, most famously as head of the Yukon detachment during the Klondike Gold Rush, and Commanding Officer of Lord Strathcona's Horse during the Boer War.

Early life

Born in Purbrook, Ontario, Canada West, he was the son of Royal Naval Captain Elmes Yelverton Steele, a veteran of the Napoleonic Wars, and his second wife, Anne Macdonald, the youngest daughter of Neil Maclain MacDonald of Ardnamurchan, a native of Islay, grandson of Captain Godfrey MacNeil of Barra and nephew of Colonel Donald MacNeil. Sam Steele received his education at the family home, Purbrooke, and then at the Royal Military College of Canada. By the age of thirteen he was orphaned, and went to live with his elder half-brother, John Steele.

Early military career

Samuel Steele's family had a strong military tradition, and in 1866 he joined the military during the Fenian Raids. Steele also participated in the Red River Expedition in 1870 to fight the Red River Rebellion of Louis Riel. Much to his disappointment, he arrived after the Métis had surrendered. The following year he joined the Permanent Force artillery, Canada's first regular army unit. Steele had long been fascinated by the West, devouring the works of James Fenimore Cooper in his youth. He was especially interested in the First Nations, and spent his time in the West learning from them and the Métis. However, he was assigned to Fort Henry in Kingston, Ontario, for the next few years, as an instructor at the Artillery School.

In 1874, Steele was initiated as a Freemason in the Lisgar Lodge No. 2, in Selkirk, Manitoba.

Life in the Mounties

In 1873, Steele was the third officer sworn in to the newly formed North-West Mounted Police (NWMP), entering as a staff constable. He was one of the officers to lead the new recruits of the NWMP on the 1874 March West, when he returned to Fort Garry, present-day Winnipeg, Manitoba. To him fell the rank of staff sergeant major and the responsibility—as an accomplished horseman and man-at-arms—of drilling the new recruits. In 1878, Steele was given his own command at Fort Qu'Appelle, Saskatchewan.

In 1877, he was assigned to meet with Sitting Bull, who, having defeated General Custer at Little Bighorn, had moved with his people into Canada to escape American vengeance. Steele along with U.S. Army General Alfred Howe Terry attempted unsuccessfully to persuade Sitting Bull to return to the United States. (Most of the Sioux did return a few years later.)

During the North-West Rebellion Steele was dispatched with a small force. Missing the Battle of Batoche the Mounties were sent to move against the last rebel force led by Big Bear. He was present at the Battle of Frenchman's Butte, where Big Bear's warriors defeated the Canadian forces under General Thomas Bland Strange. Two weeks later, Steele and his two dozen Mounties defeated Big Bear Canadian territory. The contributions of the NWMP in putting down the rebellion went largely ignored and unrewarded, to Steele's great annoyance. By 1885, Steele held the rank of superintendent. He established a NWMP station in the town of Galbraiths Ferry, which was later named to Fort Steele after Steele solved a murder in the town. He then moved on to Fort Macleod in 1888.

In 1889, at Fort Macleod, he met Marie-Elizabeth de Lotbiniere-Harwood (1859–1951), daughter of Robert William Harwood. They were married at Vaudreuil, Quebec in 1890. They had three children, including Harwood Steele, who would fictionalize episodes from his father's life in novels such as *Spirit-of-Iron* (1929).

The discovery of gold in the Klondike, Yukon, in the late 1890s presented Steele with a new challenge. Although he campaigned unsuccessfully for the position of assistant commissioner in 1892, in January 1898, he was sent to succeed Charles Constantine as commissioner and to establish customs posts at the head of the White and Chilkoot Passes, and at Lake Bennett. He was noted for his hard line with the hundreds of unruly and independent-minded prospectors, many of them American. To help control the situation, he established the rule that no one would be allowed to enter the Yukon without a ton of goods to support themselves, thus preventing the entry of desperate and potentially unruly speculators and adventurers.

Steele and his force made the Klondike Gold Rush one of the most orderly of its kind in history and made the NWMP famous around the world, which ensured its survival at a critical time when the force's dissolution was being debated in Parliament. By July 1898, Steele commanded all the NWMP in the Yukon area, and was a member of the territorial council. As the force reported directly to Ottawa, Steele had almost free rein to run things as he chose, always with an eye towards maintaining law, order and Canadian sovereignty. He moved to Dawson City in September 1898.

Boer War and second military career

Always a soldier, in 1900 Steele leapt at the offer of Canadian Pacific Railway tycoon Lord Strathcona to be the first commanding officer of Strathcona's privately-raised cavalry unit, Lord Strathcona's Horse. This Canadian light cavalry unit, in British Imperial service, was sent to South Africa during the Second Boer War, where Steele commanded them with distinction in the role of reconnaissance scouts. Steele, however, disliked greatly what he was ordered to do by the British, which included burning towns and moving the populace to concentration camps. After taking the unit back to Canada early in 1901, Steele returned to South Africa that same year to command 'B' Division of the South African Constabulary, a position he held until 1906. On his return to Canada in 1907, Steele assumed command of Military Division No. 10 (Winnipeg), where he spent his time regrouping Lord Strathcona's Horse and in preparing his memoirs.

Steele requested active military duty upon the outbreak of the First World War. He was initially rejected for command on the grounds of age. However, a compromise was reached which allowed him to act as commander of the 2nd Canadian Division until the unit was sent to France, whereupon he would be replaced. After accompanying the division to England, Steele was offered an administrative post as commanding officer of the South-East District.

Matters were complicated, however, when Canadian Minister of Defence Samuel Hughes insisted that Steele also be made commander of all Canadian troops in Europe—a slight problem, as there were two brigadier-generals who each believed the Canadian command was theirs. The issue was not resolved until 1916, when the new Minister of Overseas Military Forces of Canada, Sir G. H. Perley, removed Steele from his Canadian command after Steele refused to return to Canada as a recruiter. He kept his British command until his retirement on 15 July 1918. While in Britain, Steele was knighted, on 1 January 1918, and was made a Companion of the Most Honourable Order of the Bath, Knight Commander of the Most Distinguished Order of St. Michael and St. George, and Member of the Royal Victorian Order. Steele died of influenza just after his seventieth birthday and was later buried in Winnipeg.

Canada's fifth tallest mountain, Mount Steele, is named after him.

CFB Edmonton, the home of Lord Strathcona's Horse (Royal Canadians) is now called Steele Barracks after Major General Steele.

Personal papers

On 19 June 2008, Steele's wealth of personal papers and writings were repatriated to Canada in a ceremony in Trafalgar Square in London, England headed by Prince Edward.

Steele's papers, believed by historians to contain a wealth of heretofore untold stories that would "re-write Canadian history" had been held by British descendants of Steele, and were returned to Canada via a C$1.8MM purchase by the University of Alberta.

Source (edited): "http://en.wikipedia.org/wiki/Sam_Steele"

Victor Jory

Victor Jory (November 23, 1902 – February 12, 1982) was a Canadian actor.

Born in Dawson City, Yukon, Jory was the boxing and wrestling champion of the Coast Guard during his military service, and he kept his burly physique. He toured with theater troupes and appeared on Broadway, before making his Hollywood debut in 1930. He initially played romantic leads, but later was mostly cast as the villain. He made over 150 films and dozens of TV episodes, as well as writing two plays. His long career in radio included starring in the series *Dangerously Yours*.

He is remembered for his role as Jonas Wilkerson, the brutal and opportunistic overseer, in *Gone with the Wind* and as Lamont Cranston, aka 'The Shadow' in the 1942 serial film *The Shadow*. He also portrayed Oberon in Max Reinhardt's 1935 film adaptation of Shakespeare's play *A Midsummer Night's Dream*.

From 1959-1961, he appeared with Patrick McVey in the syndicated television police drama, *Manhunt*. Jory played the lead role of Detective Lieutenant Howard Finucane. McVey was cast as police reporter Ben Andrews.

In 1977, near the end of his career, Jory guest starred as an aging FBI agent in *The Rockford Files* episode, "The Attractive Nuisance".

For his contribution to the motion picture industry, Victor Jory has a star on the Hollywood Walk of Fame at 6605 Hollywood Blvd. He was cremated and his ashes were either given to a friend or family.

Family

Jory had two children, Jon and Jean. Jon headed the Actors Theater of Louisville, Kentucky for 31 years, building it into one of America's most respected regional theater companies. He left the job in 2000, and currently is professor of drama at the University of Washington in Seattle.

Partial filmography

Star on the Hollywood Walk of Fame at 6605 Hollywood Blvd.

- *State Fair* (1933)
- *Madame DuBarry* (1934)
- *Murder in Trinidad* (1934)
- *Party Wire* (1935)
- *A Midsummer Night's Dream* (1935)
- *Meet Nero Wolfe* (1936)
- *First Lady* (1937)
- *Glamorous Night* (1937)
- *The Adventures of Tom Sawyer* (1938)
- *Dodge City* (1939)
- *Women in the Wind* (1939)
- *Susannah of the Mounties* (1939)
- *Each Dawn I Die* (1939)
- *I Stole a Million* (1939)
- *Gone with the Wind* (1939)
- *The Shadow* (1940 serial)
- *Lady with Red Hair* (1940)
- *Secrets of the Lone Wolf* (1941)
- *Tombstone, the Town Too Tough to Die* (1942)
- *The Loves of Carmen* (1948)
- *The Capture* (1950)
- *The Cariboo Trail* (1950)
- *Cat-Women of the Moon* (1953)
- *The Man from the Alamo* (1953)
- *Valley of the Kings* (1954)
- *Blackjack Ketchum, Desperado* (1956)
- *The Man Who Turned to Stone* (1957)
- *The Last Stagecoach West* (1957)
- *The Fugitive Kind* (1959)
- *The Miracle Worker* (1962)
- *Cheyenne Autumn* (1964)
- *The Legend of Jesse James* (1966) ABC series, as Judge Parker in the episode "Things Don't Just Happen"
- *The Green Hornet* (1966)
- *F Troop* as Chief Mean Buffalo in the episode "Indian Fever", ABC series (1966)
- *The Road West* in episode "Beyond the Hill", NBC series (1967)
- *The Time Tunnel* in episode "Pirates Of Deadman's Island", ABC series (1967)
- *Mackenna's Gold* as Narrator (1969)
- *A Time for Dying* (1969)
- *Papillon* (1973)
- *The Mountain Men* (1980)
- *The Puppetoon Movie* (1987)

Source (edited): "http://en.wikipedia.org/wiki/Victor_Jory"

William Judge

Father William Judge was a Jesuit priest who during the 1897 Klondike Gold Rush established St. Mary's Hospital, a facility in Dawson which provided shelter, food and any available medicine to the many hard-at-luck gold miners who filled the town and its environs.

Judge's humanitarian work became known due to the writings of Jack London, whose health — and possibly his life — was saved by the priest. As later described by himself, London — like many others involved in the Gold Rush — became malnourished and developed scurvy. His gums became swollen, eventually leading to the loss of his four front teeth. A constant gnawing pain affected his abdomen and leg muscles, and his face was stricken with sores. Due to Judge's ministrations, he and many others recovered their health.

Judge became known as "The Saint of Dawson", but up to the present this remains an unofficial nickname.

Source (edited): "http://en.wikipedia.org/wiki/William_Judge"

William L. Walsh

of King George V's silver jubilee. Sitting (L to R): Edmonton mayor Joseph Clarke, Lieutenant Governor William L. Walsh, Mrs. Walsh, Chief Justice of the Supreme Court of Alberta Horace Harvey. Standing (L to R): Col. P. Anderson, Col. F. C. Jamieson, Lt. Day, Capt. Sims, Reid.

William Legh Walsh, KC (January 28, 1857 – January 13, 1938) was a Canadian lawyer and judge. He served as the fourth Lieutenant Governor of Alberta from 1931 to 1936.

He was born in Simcoe, Ontario, the son of Aquila Walsh, a member of the Canadian House of Commons. He studied law at the University of Toronto and Osgoode Hall, was called to the bar in 1880 and practiced law in Orangeville. In 1900, he went to the Yukon and practiced law in Dawson City during the Klondike Gold Rush. In 1903, he was named King's Counsel.

He moved to Calgary in 1904 and joined a law firm there. He became the first President of the Conservative Association of Alberta in 1905. In 1912, he was appointed to the Supreme Court of Alberta and served until he became lieutenant governor in 1931.

He died in Victoria, British Columbia in 1938, aged 80.

William Walsh had two children, a son and a daughter. His son Legh Aquila Walsh was born in 1895. He enlisted in the Canadian Expeditionary Force during World War One and served the duration of the war. At the time of his enlistment he described his occupation as law student. He became a Lieutenant in the 82nd Battalion in May 1916. He was wounded at Courcelette in 1916, returned briefly to Calgary, and then sailed back to the front. After the war he returned to Calgary in April 1919.

His daughter Marguerite (also known as Greta) married Dr. George Robinson Pirie (1879-1938), a prominent children's doctor and member of the Royal College of Physicians (1931). They were married in Calgary on April 14th, 1909. He was Superintendent of the Great Ormond Street children's hospital in England from 1914-1919. They had one child, Miss Margaret Walsh Pirie (Mrs. R. O. Funston).

Source (edited): "http://en.wikipedia.org/wiki/William_L._Walsh"

William Ogilvie (surveyor)

William Ogilvie FRGS (Ottawa, April 7, 1846–Winnipeg, Manitoba, November 13, 1912), was a Canadian Dominion land surveyor, explorer and Commissioner of the Yukon Territory.

He was born on a farm in Gloucester Township, Canada West in an area now known as Glen Ogilvie to James Ogilvie of Belfast Ireland and Margaret Holliday Ogilvie of Peebles, Scotland. Ogilvie articled as a surveyor with Robert Sparks, qualifying to practice as a Provincial Land Surveyor in 1869. He married Sparks' daughter Mary, a school teacher, in 1872. He worked locally as a land surveyor, qualified as a Dominion Land Surveyor in 1872 and was first hired by the Dominion government in 1875.

He was responsible for numerous surveys from the 1870s to the 1890s, mainly in the Prairie Provinces. From 1887 to 1889, Ogilvie was involved in George Mercer Dawson's exploration and survey expedition in what later became the Yukon Territory. He surveyed the Chilkoot Pass, the Yukon and Porcupine rivers. Ogilvie established the location of the boundary between the Yukon and Alaska on the 141st meridian west.

During the Klondike Gold Rush, he surveyed the townsite of Dawson City and was responsible for settling many disputes between miners. Ogilvie became the Yukon's second Commissioner in 1898 at the height of the gold rush, and resigned because of ill-health in 1901.

He was the author of *Early Days on the Yukon* (1913), which is still available in facsimile reprints. The Ogilvie Mountains, Ogilvie River and Ogilvie Aerodrome in the Northern Yukon Territory along with Ogilvie Valley in the Southern Yukon Territory are named after him.

Ogilvie performed the following surveys for the Surveyor-General of Canada:

1875 - 76—Township outlines south of Dauphin.
1878 - 79—Surveys of Indian Reserves, Bow River.
1880—Township outlines West of York.
1881 -- Fourth meridian to Township 40.
1882—Seventh base line West of Fourth meridian.

1883 -- Fifth meridian from Edmonton to Athabaska River and Twenty-first base line Westerly.
1884—Micrometer survey of Peace River from Chipewyan to Dunvegan and Athabaska River from Slave River to Athabaska Landing.
1885—Traverse along C.P.R. in British Columbia.
1887—Exploration surveys—Yukon River and Mackenzie River.
1888 - 89—Surveys and explorations—Porcupine, Lewes, Bell, Trout and Peel River.
1890—Exploration survey between Lake Temiscamingue and Hudson Bay.
1891—Examination between Liard and Peace Rivers.
1892—Subdivision and re-surveys in Prince Albert District.
Source (edited): "http://en.wikipedia.org/wiki/William_Ogilvie_(surveyor)"